THE SOLAR SYSTEM

MARS

A MyReportLinks.com Book

STEPHEN FEINSTEIN

MyReportLinks.com Books

an imprint of

 Enslow Publishers, Inc.

Box 398, 40 Industrial Road
Berkeley Heights, NJ 07922
USA

MyReportLinks.com Books, an imprint of Enslow Publishers, Inc. MyReportLinks®
is a registered trademark of Enslow Publishers, Inc.

Library of Congress Cataloging-in-Publication Data

Feinstein, Stephen.
   Mars / Stephen Feinstein.
      p. cm. — (The solar system)
   Includes bibliographical references and index.
   ISBN 0-7660-5302-4
   1. Mars (Planet)—Juvenile literature. I. Title. II. Solar system (Berkeley Heights, N.J.)
   QB641.F35 2005
   523.43--dc22
                                    2004015886

Printed in the United States of America

10 9 8 7 6 5 4 3 2 1

To Our Readers:
Through the purchase of this book, you and your library gain access to the Report Links that specifically back
up this book.
The Publisher will provide access to the Report Links that back up this book and will keep these Report Links
up to date on **www.myreportlinks.com** for five years from the book's first publication date.
We have done our best to make sure all Internet addresses in this book were active and appropriate when we went
to press. However, the author and the Publisher have no control over, and assume no liability for, the material
available on those Internet sites or on other Web sites they may link to.
The usage of the MyReportLinks.com Books Web site is subject to the terms and conditions stated on the Usage
Policy Statement on **www.myreportlinks.com**.
A password may be required to access the Report Links that back up this book. The password is found on the
bottom of page 4 of this book.
Any comments or suggestions can be sent by e-mail to comments@myreportlinks.com or to the address on the
back cover.

Photo Credits: © Nicolaus Copernicus Museum, p. 13; © Windows to the Universe, pp. 12, 17; European Space
Agency, pp. 28, 33; Library of Congress, pp. 18, 19; Lunar and Planetary Institute, p. 23; MyReportLinks.com
Books, p. 4; National Aeronautics and Space Administration (NASA), pp. 1, 3, 9, 10, 15, 20, 22, 25, 27, 30, 35,
37, 38, 40, 42, 43; Photos.com, pp. 3, 9.

Note: Some NASA photos were only available in a low-resolution format.

Cover Photo: National Aeronautics and Space Administration.

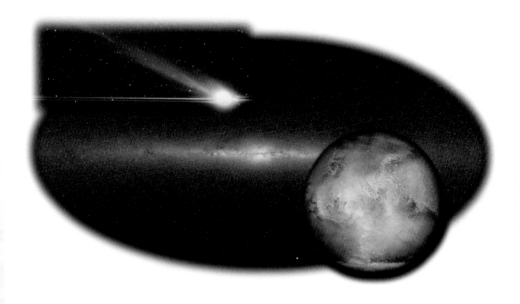

MyReportLinks.com Books
Great Books, Great Links, Great for Research!

The Internet sites listed on the next four pages can save you hours of research time. These Internet sites—we call them "Report Links"—are constantly changing, but we keep them up to date on our Web site.

Give it a try! Type http://www.myreportlinks.com into your browser, click on the series title, then the book title, and scroll down to the Report Links listed for this book.

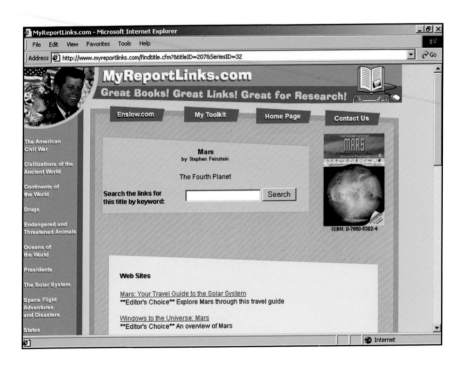

The Report Links will bring you to great source documents, photographs, and illustrations. MyReportLinks.com Books save you time, feature Report Links that are kept up to date, and make report writing easier than ever!

Please see "To Our Readers" on the copyright page for important information about this book, the MyReportLinks.com Web site, and the Report Links that back up this book.

Please enter **PMR1912** if asked for a password.

Report Links

The Internet sites described below can be accessed at
http://www.myreportlinks.com

*EDITOR'S CHOICE

▶**Mars: Your Travel Guide to the Solar System**
From the BBC comes a site with basic information, videos, pictures,
and links to other resources about Mars. The site also contains links
to many other sites about the solar system.

*EDITOR'S CHOICE

▶**Windows to the Universe: Mars**
This Web site offers a great deal of information about Mars, including
facts about the interior and surface of the planet, its atmosphere,
its moons, and more.

*EDITOR'S CHOICE

▶**Nineplanets.org: Mars**
Learn about the planet Mars, the fourth planet from the Sun, from
this site. Information on its orbit, terrain, atmosphere, satellites,
and more is included.

*EDITOR'S CHOICE

▶**Welcome to the Planets: Mars**
This NASA site offers images of the terrain on Mars, including some
showing canyons, volcanoes, craters, chasmas, and weather patterns.

*EDITOR'S CHOICE

▶**NASA's Mars Exploration Program**
This is one of NASA's key Web sites for the study of Mars. Extensive
information can be found on all missions to the planet, as well as news,
events, and facts.

*EDITOR'S CHOICE

▶**Mars**
This NASA site provides a look at the Red Planet and offers a time line
of all missions to Mars, beginning with the first flyby in 1964.

Any comments? Contact us: **comments@myreportlinks.com**   5

Peabody Public Library
Columbia City, IN

Report Links

▶ Ask an Astronomer for Kids: Mars

Mars, the Red Planet, has long fascinated us. This site offers interesting information about the planet, including why it appears red.

▶ The Case for Mars

This site offers a collection of summaries of articles about Mars. It also provides links to more information about the possibility of humans exploring and colonizing Mars.

▶ Center for Mars Exploration

This NASA site provides a wide range of information on Mars, including digital atlases, three-dimensional images, videos, essays, and many other photographs.

▶ Drive on Mars

This site comes from an expert in the field of virtual technology. It offers the opportunity to explore Mars in a virtual rover over digital Martian terrain. The software used by this site is also used by NASA in its space programs.

▶ Explore Mars Now

This site gives you the opportunity to explore a virtual base and rover on Mars through a Web-based simulator. Read the text as you move through the rooms, and learn as you have fun.

▶ Exploring Mars

Learn about Mars, the Red Planet, from this comprehensive site. Included is information on Mars exploration, weather, climate, missions, and maps.

▶ Exploring the Planets: Mars

This Web site from the Smithsonian's National Air and Space Museum provides facts and images about Mars. Information is also provided on the Viking missions to Mars.

▶ Just for Kids!

This NASA site mixes learning and fun while aiming to teach kids about the planet Mars. Games include one in which viewers create their own missions and make topographical maps.

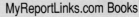
Report Links

The Internet sites described below can be accessed at
http://www.myreportlinks.com

▶Mars Dead or Alive

This PBS site includes an interview with the scientist who originally came up
with the idea for the Mars Exploration Rover vehicles. Images, interactive
features, and videos are also included.

▶Mars Exploration: Fun Zone

Designed for kids, this NASA site offers a number of games and activities that
will help students learn more about Mars.

▶Mars *Express*

Until the Mars *Express* mission, Europeans had never sent a spacecraft to Mars.
On June 2, 2003, the *Beagle 2* set off for Mars but did not land there. On the
European Space Agency's site, find out more about this mission.

▶Mars *Global Surveyor* Images of the Cydonia Region of Mars

This NASA site is a collection of images of the infamous "face" on Mars located
in the Cydonia region of the planet. Some people believe it is proof that Mars
was once inhabited by humans.

▶Mars Institute

You will learn how the Mars Institute is trying to further the scientific study,
exploration, and public understanding of Mars when you visit the group's
Web site.

▶Mars Introduction

This site offers statistical information about Mars as well as images of the Red
Planet. Information on its atmosphere and moons is included, along with a
number of animations.

▶Mars Now

This California Space Institute Web site features a research library filled with
resources on the Red Planet, including an interactive learning museum.

▶Mars Rover Special Report

This site is a collection of articles and resources that focus on NASA's robotic
Rover vehicles, which are busy exploring Mars.

Report Links

The Internet sites described below can be accessed at http://www.myreportlinks.com

▶The Mars Society
At this site, learn about one of the key organizations behind the push for human exploration and settlement of Mars.

▶Mission to Mars
The Mars Exploration Rovers (MER), named *Spirit* and *Opportunity*, have a lot of work to do on Mars. On this site, read the Rover journal and view some of the pictures the robotic vehicles have sent back to Earth.

▶Mission to Mars: A Special Report
More information on the Mars Rovers is offered at this site. Learn about the vehicles themselves, get up-to-date news about the mission, and view exciting images from Mars.

▶Nicolaus Copernicus Museum, Frombork
Take a virtual tour of the life of the sixteenth-century Polish astronomer at this museum Web site. Copernicus brought about a revolution in astronomical science by arguing for the heliocentric theory.

▶The Planetary Society: Exploring Mars
This site provides extensive information on Mars, including government-sponsored missions, exploration of Mars by the private sector, facts about Mars, and an interesting time line.

▶*The War of the Worlds*
The full text of H.G. Wells's classic science-fiction novel is available at this site. This nineteenth-century tale of Martians landing on Earth was later adapted as a radio broadcast, creating fear and panic among listeners who thought the landing was real.

▶What We Know About the Red Planet
A lot of interesting information on Mars is offered at this site. An entire section is dedicated to missions to the planet, and there are also links to other resources.

▶Why Is Mars Red, and Is There Any Life on the Planet?
This BBC site explains why the Red Planet is red and discusses whether any evidence of life exists on Mars. Also included is information on the biggest volcano in the solar system, which happens to be on Mars.

Any comments? Contact us: **comments@myreportlinks.com**

Mars Facts

Age
About 4.5 billion years

Diameter at Equator
4,219 miles (6,794 kilometers)

Composition
Iron core, mantle, and crust of various rock

Average Distance From the Sun
About 142 million miles (228 million kilometers)

Closest Approach to Earth
About 35 million miles (56 million kilometers)

Orbital Period (year, in Earth days)
687 days

Rotational Period (day, in Earth hours)
24 hours 39 minutes

Mass (percent of Earth's mass)
10.74 percent

Atmosphere
95.3 percent carbon dioxide, with small amounts of nitrogen and argon
Mars's atmosphere is about 100 times less dense than Earth's.

Temperature
Average daytime: −22°F (−30°C)
Average nighttime: −148°F (−100°C)
Highest (ground level in summer at equator): 72°F (22°C)
Lowest (winter at south pole): −193°F (−125°C)

Number of Moons
Two (Deimos and Phobos)

Surface Gravity
38 percent of Earth's gravity

Chapter 1 ▶

The Red Planet

Mars, the fourth planet from the Sun, is the next planet beyond Earth's orbit. While Venus, a scorching hot and poisonous world, is the nearest planet to Earth, Mars is more like our own planet than any other planet in the solar system. Both planets were formed about 4.5 billion years ago.

Like Earth, Venus, and Mercury, Mars is known as a "terrestrial," or Earth-like, planet, made of rock and metal. With a diameter of 4,219 miles (6,794 kilometers), Mars is slightly more than half the size of Earth. While Earth has one Moon, Mars has two—Deimos and Phobos. Mars can easily be seen in Earth's skies.

Both Mars and Earth have atmospheres, although the atmosphere of Mars is much thinner than that of Earth. Both planets have polar ice caps. But since Mars is farther away from the Sun than Earth is, it is colder than our world, although in the distant past, Mars may have been warmer and much more like Earth. Recent discoveries on Mars have led scientists to think that there

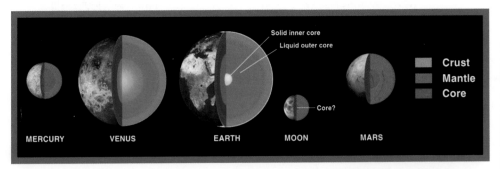

▲ In this diagram showing the compositions of the terrestrial planets and Earth's Moon, Mars is the last planet pictured.

was once liquid water on the surface of Mars. If that proves to be true, then it is possible that life may have existed there also.

Mars, God of War

Mars has captured the imagination of human beings for thousands of years. The planet's distinctive fiery reddish-orange color, which led Mars to be called the Red Planet, also inspired awe and wonder as people watched Mars in the night skies. The reddish color of Mars is caused by a layer of dust on the surface that is rich in iron oxide, or rust. Strong winds kick up huge dust storms that envelop parts of the planet and cause reddish-pink smog to form in the Martian atmosphere.

As people observed this mysterious red beacon in the sky, images of blood and fire came to mind. The Red Planet became a symbol of war for the ancient Sumerians. The Babylonians believed that Nergal, their god of death and disease, lived on the Red Planet. According to an ancient Babylonian text, "When Nergal is dim, it is lucky; when bright, unlucky."[1]

Down through the centuries, various peoples continued to identify the Red Planet with their gods of war. The ancient Persians called the planet Pahlavani Siphir. The Egyptians called it Harmakhis. The Greeks named the planet Ares after their god of war, and the Romans did the same, calling it Mars, the name we still use.

Mars, the god of war, represented the triumphal military spirit of the Roman Empire. According to Roman legend, Mars was the father of Romulus and Remus, the founders of Rome. The Romans coined the word *martial* to refer to combat and the arts of war. And they named the third day of the week Mars-day. Today, many peoples still name the third day of the week after the ancient god of war. The French call it *mardi,* and the Italians call it *martedi.*[2] The English word *Tuesday* comes from the Anglo-Saxon *Tiwes daeg,* which in turn came from *Tui,* the ancient Norse war god and the name the Norse gave to the Red Planet.

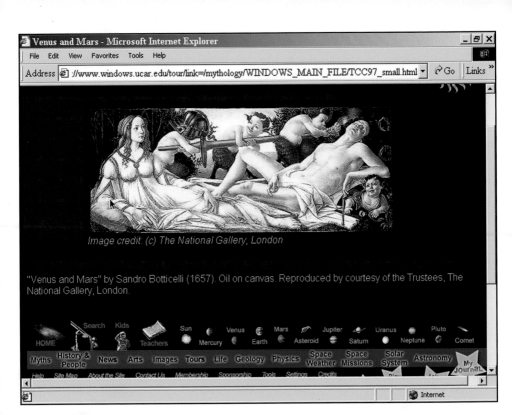

"Venus and Mars" by Sandro Botticelli (1657). Oil on canvas. Reproduced by courtesy of the Trustees, The National Gallery, London.

▲ Two central figures in Roman mythology—Venus, the goddess of love and beauty, and Mars, the god of war—are the subjects of this seventeenth-century painting.

As recently as the Middle Ages in Europe, most people still believed that the planets and stars controlled the fate of humankind. Mars was thought to have an especially powerful effect. Astrologers claimed that they could predict the outcomes of single battles and even entire wars by studying the movements of Mars. The royal astrologer would check Mars's position in the sky before advising the king when to attack an enemy. According to a fifteenth-century German manuscript on astrology, "Mars rules catastrophes and war, it is master of the daylight hours of Tuesday and the hours of darkness on Friday, its element is the fire, its metal is iron, its gems jasper and hematite. Its qualities are warm and dry, it rules the color red, the liver, the blood vessels, the kidneys and the gallbladder as well as the left ear. Being of choleric temper it especially rules males between the ages of 42 and 57."[3]

Astronomers Study Mars

In ancient times, most people believed that Earth was a stationary body around which all the heavenly bodies revolved. This seemed common sense. Anyone who looked up in the sky could see that the Sun, Moon, planets, and stars moved across the sky, sank below the horizon, and reappeared the next day. Nobody could feel Earth spinning on its axis or speeding on its path around the Sun. However, in ancient Greece in around the year 270 B.C., Aristarchus of Samos came to a different conclusion after making

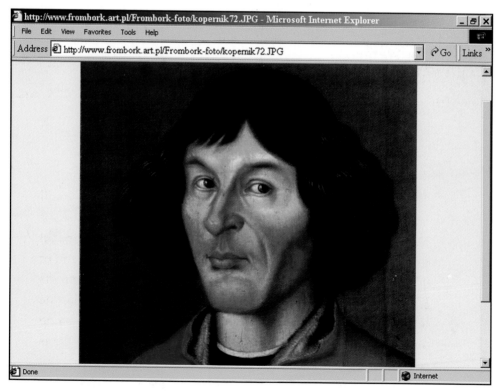

▲ The sixteenth-century Polish astronomer Nicolaus Copernicus, who was convinced that Mars and the other planets revolved around the Sun, brought about a revolution in astronomical science.

careful observations of the heavens. He came to believe that not only was the Sun much larger than Earth, but also that the Sun was at the center of the solar system, with all the planets, including Earth, revolving around it. Not surprisingly, most of the other astronomers of his day ignored the heliocentric, or Sun-centered, theory of Aristarchus.

The second-century A.D. Greek astronomer Claudius Ptolemy wrote a complex, detailed description of a geocentric, or Earth-centered universe, which reinforced what most people believed. Ptolemy's views went nearly unchallenged until 1543. That year, the Polish astronomer Nicolaus Copernicus published *On the Revolution of the Heavenly Spheres* in which he revived Aristarchus' idea of a universe with the Sun at its center. Copernicus argued so convincingly for the heliocentric theory that he ushered in a revolution in astronomical science. It eventually became accepted fact that the Sun is the center of the solar system, while Earth and the other planets rotate on their axes as they travel around the Sun. Even so, the famous American astronomer Carl Sagan pointed out that we still refer to the Sun rising and setting even though it does neither. As Sagan said, "It is 2,200 years since Aristarchus, and our language still pretends that the Earth does not turn."[4]

▶ Mars Through a Lens

In 1610, Galileo Galilei became the first person to look at Mars through a telescope. Because Mars shines by reflected sunlight, as Earth's Moon does, it shows distinct phases depending on its position in relation to the positions of Earth and the Sun. Mars never appears as a crescent like Earth's Moon, however. Believing that he had observed the phases of Mars, Galileo wrote, "I ought not to claim that I can see the phases of Mars; however, unless I am deceiving myself, I believe I have already seen that he is not perfectly round."[5]

As the use of telescopes became more widespread, improvements were made in their design. Astronomers began to notice

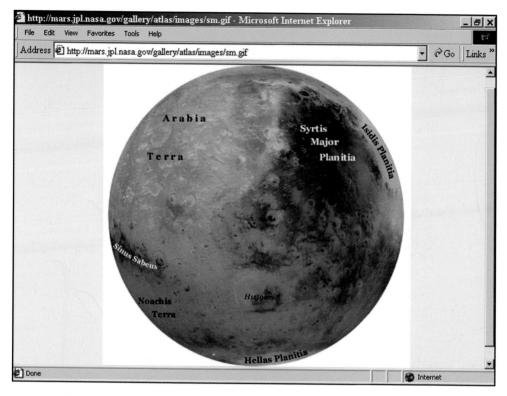

```
http://mars.jpl.nasa.gov/gallery/atlas/images/sm.gif - Microsoft Internet Explorer
File   Edit   View   Favorites   Tools   Help
Address   http://mars.jpl.nasa.gov/gallery/atlas/images/sm.gif          Go   Links »
```

Arabia

Terra

Syrtis
Major
Planitia

Isidis Planitia

Sinus Sabeus

Noachis
Terra

Huygens

Hellas Planitia

Done   Internet

This view of Mars features Syrtis Major, a large, dark volcanic region that was first identified through a telescope in 1659 by the Dutch astronomer Christiaan Huygens. Formerly called the Kaiser Sea, it extends 930 miles (1,500 kilometers) north from the planet's equator. The word syrtis *refers to quicksand.*

the surface features of Mars. In 1659, the Dutch astronomer Christiaan Huygens studied Mars carefully through a telescope. He discovered a huge triangular-shaped dark area, now called Syrtis Major, on the Martian surface. By observing how long it took for the dark area to reappear after it had disappeared from view, Huygens concluded that Mars rotates on its axis and that the Martian day is about twenty-four hours long, almost the same as the length of a day on Earth.

In 1666, an Italian astronomer named Giovanni Cassini discovered that Mars, like Earth, has polar ice caps. Six years later, he was able to calculate the distance from Earth to Mars at about 50 million miles (80 million kilometers). The actual distance varies from about 35 million miles to 63 million miles (56 million kilometers to 101 million kilometers). In 1777, the British astronomer William Herschel discovered that Mars's axis of rotation is tilted at almost the same angle as Earth's axis. Based on this finding, Herschel concluded that Mars, like Earth, has four seasons. In 1784, he noticed that Mars's polar ice caps grew and shrank with the seasons. He also decided that changes in the brightness of the planet could be caused by clouds in Mars's atmosphere and that the dark areas on the surface of Mars were seas. Before long, Herschel and others were speculating about the existence of life on Mars as well as life on other planets. Herschel concluded that Mars's inhabitants "probably enjoy a situation in many respects similar to our own."[6]

▶ The "Canals" of Mars: Signs of Life?

In 1860, a French astronomer named Emmanuel Liais suggested that the dark areas on Mars were areas of vegetation rather than seas, because they seemed to change color with the seasons. Others disagreed, maintaining that the existence of seas and continents had already been proven.

In 1878, those who believed that Mars could be inhabited received new support for their beliefs. That year, the Italian astronomer Giovanni Schiaparelli observed a series of forty dark lines on the surface of Mars. Schiaparelli called them *canali,* which translates as "channels," but others misinterpreted *canali* as "canals," which are artificially made waterways. Although Schiaparelli believed the canali to be the result of some natural, but as yet unknown, geological process, those hoping for signs of Martian life were encouraged.

The French astronomer Nicolas Camille Flammarion, who supported Schiaparelli's idea of Martian channels, also believed that intelligent life existed on Mars. In 1892, Flammarion wrote

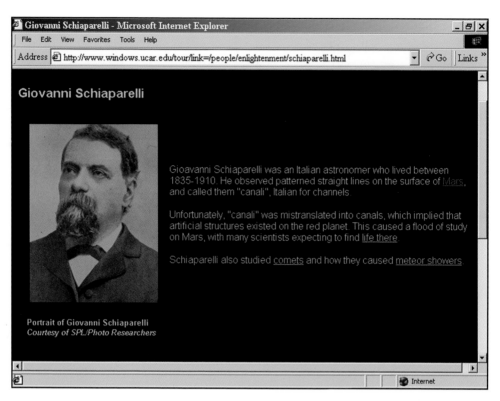

Giovanni Schiaparelli - Microsoft Internet Explorer

File   Edit   View   Favorites   Tools   Help

Address ⬚ http://www.windows.ucar.edu/tour/link=/people/enlightenment/schiaparelli.html   ⬡ Go   Links »

Giovanni Schiaparelli

Gioavanni Schiaparelli was an Italian astronomer who lived between 1835-1910. He observed patterned straight lines on the surface of Mars, and called them "canali", Italian for channels.

Unfortunately, "canali" was mistranslated into canals, which implied that artificial structures existed on the red planet. This caused a flood of study on Mars, with many scientists expecting to find life there.

Schiaparelli also studied comets and how they caused meteor showers.

Portrait of Giovanni Schiaparelli
Courtesy of SPL/Photo Researchers

⬢ Internet

The Italian astronomer Giovanni Schiaparelli observed patterned lines on Mars that he called canali, *Italian for "channels." His term was mistakenly translated as "canals," leading some to believe that artificial structures existed on the Red Planet, which meant that intelligent life must once have existed there, too.*

" . . . because the world of Mars is older than ours, mankind there will be more advanced and wiser."[7] Flammarion and many other astronomers of the time believed that the planets in the solar system had formed in stages rather than all around the same time.

▷ The Search for Intelligent Life

Samuel Phelps Leland, an astronomy professor at Charles City College in Iowa, was an enthusiastic believer in the existence of intelligent life on Mars. In 1898, he wrote that the new powerful telescopes would soon enable astronomers "to see cities on Mars, to detect navies in its harbors and the smoke of great manufacturing

In 1898, with the publication of his science-fiction novel The War of the Worlds, *the English author H. G. Wells helped to fuel speculation that Mars was inhabited.*

cities and towns. . . . Is Mars inhabited? There can be little doubt of it. . . . Is it possible to know this of a certainty? Certainly."[8] That year, the English writer H. G. Wells published *The War of the Worlds* in which Earth is invaded by a hostile and tech-nologically superior race of Martians. Many other writers would create stories about Mars and Martians in the years to come.

In 1905, American astronomer Percival Lowell produced a map of Mars showing five times as many channels as Schiaparelli had found. Lowell reasoned that since the channels were straight lines, they must be artificial since straight lines do not appear in nature. In 1895, Lowell had met with Flammarion in Paris. The French astronomer told Lowell that it had been established beyond a doubt that water from the Martian poles flows through the channels. Lowell then visited Schiaparelli in Milan. By this time, Schiaparelli was coming around to the view that intelligent beings might be responsible for the channels. As for Lowell, he was convinced that the channels were actually a network of canals built by intelligent beings. Their purpose was to transport water from the polar ice caps to Mars's desert regions.

The idea that the surface of Mars was crisscrossed by a network of canals built by intelligent Martians fired up the imagination of science-fiction writers. Those writers did not care that most scientists did not believe in the existence of Martian canals nor did they believe that life existed on the Red Planet. In 1907, the biologist Alfred Russel Wallace had written that "Mars not only is not inhabited by intelligent beings such as Mr. Lowell postulates, but is absolutely UNINHABITABLE."[9] Wallace's words failed to dampen the enthusiasm of the science-fiction writers. They were far more interested in Lowell's comment that "Extraterrestrial life does not necessarily mean extraterrestrial human life. Under changed conditions, life itself must take on other forms."[10]

Soon, writers were coming up with stories about bug-eyed monsters and little green men from Mars. On October 30, 1938, the famous American director, actor, and writer Orson Welles stunned millions of Americans when he did a radio broadcast of H. G. Wells's *War of the Worlds*. The broadcast, in the format of a news report, described the landing of Martian invaders in New Jersey. But most listeners missed the introductory comments explaining that the broadcast was adapted from a work of fiction. Widespread panic occurred

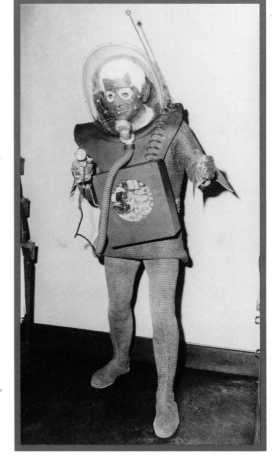

The public preoccupation with Martians in the 1940s and 1950s can be seen in this costume based on a Martian character in a science-fiction thriller.

▲ *This is the first photograph taken on the surface of Mars, showing small and large rocks and the fine grains of Martian soil.* Viking 1 *provided this image shortly after it landed on the planet's surface on July 20, 1976.*

in many parts of the country as people thought the invasion was for real.

Next, films depicted trips to Mars and invasions of Earth by Martians. Millions of people flocked to see *Rocketship XM, Invaders From Mars, Robinson Crusoe on Mars,* and a film version of *The War of the Worlds.* In the popular imagination, a Mars that was inhabited by intelligent beings had become a very real possibility.

Then in the 1960s, the United States sent unmanned Mariner space probes to Mars. *Mariner 4,* the first of these to successfully reach the Red Planet, arrived at Mars in July 1965. *Mariner 4* sent back close-up photos of the Martian surface that revealed old, eroded impact craters, like those on the Moon. But there were no canals and certainly no signs of Martian life—intelligent or otherwise. The straight dark lines seen by Schiaparelli and Lowell were nowhere to be found. The astronomers who thought they had observed canals had probably seen shadows and spots on Mars and had misinterpreted them as straight lines.

The fanciful theories of Martian canals and Martians were dealt a severe blow. But was the Red Planet truly a dead planet? The quest to discover whether life had ever existed on Mars was just beginning.

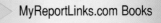
Chapter 2 ▶

Our Cold, Dry Neighbor

When astronomers first began using telescopes to study Mars, they thought that the Red Planet was like Earth in many ways. Mars seemed to have an atmosphere, it had polar ice caps, and it might have water. Astronomers concluded that Mars had seasons because of the tilt of its axis and easily seen changes in brightness. They believed dark areas on the surface were seas. Some had interpreted surface markings on Mars to be canals built by intelligent beings. The similarities between Mars and Earth led many astronomers to believe that the Red Planet might be inhabited. We now know that, despite some similarities, Mars is very different from Earth.

▶ Unbreathable Air, Dangerous Radiation

As far as we know, Earth is the only planet in the solar system where conditions were suitable for life to develop, evolve, and thrive. Mars may have had a favorable environment for life early in its history, perhaps 2 billion or 3 billion years ago. But the Red Planet of today is hostile to most life as we know it, except perhaps forms of microbes that can exist in extreme environments.

If humans were to travel to Mars, land on the planet, and set out to explore the surface, they would need to wear protective space suits to survive. Mars's atmosphere is thin—less than one hundredth the density of Earth's. There is no protective ozone layer as on Earth, so an unprotected person would be exposed to dangerous levels of ultraviolet radiation from the Sun. Also, humans could not breathe Martian air, because it consists of about 95.3 percent carbon dioxide, 2.7 percent nitrogen, 1.6 percent argon, and only 0.2 percent oxygen.[1]

Mars's gravitational field is not much more than a third of Earth's. Perhaps that is why Mars's atmosphere is so thin. The Red Planet may have had a thicker atmosphere at one time, but the weak gravitational field may have allowed much of the gases to escape. Mars's gravity, 38 percent of Earth's, would make it easier for humans to explore the Red Planet, though. A person weighing 100 pounds (45 kilograms) on Earth would weigh only about 38 pounds (17 kilograms) on Mars.

Like Earth, Mars has weather patterns that include clouds and prevailing winds. But the similarity ends there. On Mars, the skies are never blue but are always pink from the dust in the atmosphere. Although there are thin clouds in the Martian atmosphere, there is not enough water vapor for precipitation. So it never rains or snows on Mars, although it might have long ago. Much of the Red Planet is barren desert, swept by ferocious dust storms. At times, strong winds envelop the planet in reddish dust. Such storms have been known to last for several months. Dust clouds occur up to 12 miles (19 kilometers) above the surface. Above the dust are clouds of ice crystals (frozen water). At about

▲ This photograph of a dune field in the Endurance Crater highlights the reddish dust of this part of the Red Planet. Dunes are a common surface feature on Mars.

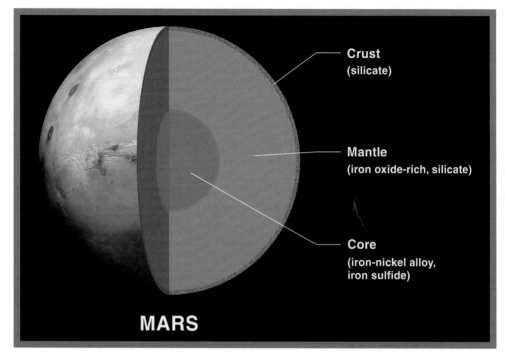

MARS

⚠️ *Because Mars is about half the size of Earth, scientists believe the Red Planet's center has cooled much more than Earth's core has. They think that Mars is mostly made up of rock and metal.*

18 miles (30 kilometers) above the surface is another layer of hazy dust. And at about 30 miles (50 kilometers) above the surface are ice clouds (frozen carbon dioxide).

Humans on Mars would need to be protected from dust storms and also from the low temperatures. Most of the time it is extremely cold, much colder than on Earth, because Mars is farther from the Sun than Earth is, and Mars's thin atmosphere does not provide much insulation. The average temperature in the daytime is −22°F (−30°C), and the average temperature at night is −148°F (−100°C). While noontime temperatures in summer near the Martian equator can reach as high as 72°F (22°C) at ground level, winter temperatures near the planet's south pole can fall to −193°F (−125°C). At this temperature, carbon dioxide freezes, and the ice cap at the south pole is believed to be made up mostly of frozen carbon dioxide.

How Mars Was Formed

Scientists believe that the Sun and the planets of the solar system formed about 4.5 billion years ago. The force of gravity pulled together hydrogen gas and dust particles floating in the space between the stars into a spinning disk. The Sun formed first at the center of the disk. Then the planets formed out of dust and clumps of rocky debris circling the Sun. The infant Mars grew larger as its gravitational pull attracted rocks and dust that crossed its orbital path. As Mars grew larger, it became hotter, so its rocky material melted. The heavier elements, mainly iron, sank to the center of Mars and became the planet's core. Eventually, Mars began to cool.

What Mars Is Made Of

Mars's structure is made up of three main layers—the iron core, the mantle, and the crust. Mars's core is proportionately much smaller than Earth's. The core of Mars, with a radius of 680 miles (1,100 kilometers), makes up only about 6 percent of the planet's mass. In contrast, Earth's core makes up 32 percent of its mass. Scientists believe that Mars either has a solid core or a liquid core with slow-moving currents and that this may explain why the planet has a weak magnetic field. Mars's mantle, which is about 1,400 miles (2,300 kilometers) deep, is less dense than the core. The mantle is solid and contains silica. The rocky crust, which rests on the mantle, is about 30 miles (50 kilometers) deep.

The Highest Volcanoes and the Deepest Canyons

The surface of Mars includes some of the most spectacular scenery in the solar system. The southern two thirds of Mars is made up of highlands, while the northern third is lowlands. Early

The Martian volcano Olympus Mons is by far the largest volcano in all the solar system. It is about 100 times larger in volume than Mauna Loa, the largest volcano on Earth.

in its history, Mars was subjected to the same heavy bombardment by asteroids and meteors as the other terrestrial planets. This period ended about 3.8 billion years ago. The heavily cratered surface of the highlands, with the same kinds of features found on Mercury and the Moon, is evidence of the bombardment. An impact basin on Mars known as Hellas Planitia may be the largest impact basin in the solar system, with a diameter of about 1,200 miles (2,000 kilometers). There are not many craters in the northern third of Mars's surface. Volcanic eruptions and floods in the northern part of the planet erased evidence of the bombardment. Instead, the northern third of Mars consists mainly of smooth lava plains.

The Tharsis Rise

An area called the Tharsis Rise forms a tremendous bulge between the lowlands and the highlands. The Tharsis Rise is about 6 miles (10 kilometers) high and about 5,000 miles (8,000 kilometers) across. Although plate tectonics (the shifting of large slabs of land responsible for much of Earth's earthquake activity) is absent on Mars, the Red Planet has been fractured and faulted in many areas, especially in the Tharsis Rise region. Wrinkle ridges, formed by tectonic action, occur in the volcanic plains surrounding the Tharsis Rise.

The Tharsis Rise is also the area of greatest volcanic activity on Mars. Scientists believe that although most of this activity happened in Mars's distant past, some volcanic activity may still be occurring somewhere on the planet.

Enormous shield volcanoes that dwarf Earth's tallest mountains and volcanoes rise high into the Martian sky from the Tharsis area. The largest of these, Olympus Mons, is more than 16 miles (26 kilometers) high and 375 miles (603 kilometers) across. By comparison, Mount Everest, Earth's highest mountain, is only about 5.5 miles (9 kilometers) high. Olympus Mons is the largest volcano in the solar system. If Olympus Mons were located on Earth in the area of the Cascade Mountains in the northwestern United States, it would cover all of Washington State and half of Oregon. A chain of huge volcanoes stretches across the center of the Tharsis Rise. Three of them are more than 12 miles (19 kilometers) high.

The Tharsis Rise is also the site of Valles Marineris (Mariner Valley), the largest canyon system in the solar system. Valles Marineris is named after the Mariner space probes that reached Mars in the 1960s. It is up to 5 miles (8 kilometers) deep in places, 300 miles (483 kilometers) wide, and 2,800 miles (4,505 kilometers) long.[2] If Valles Marineris were located on Earth in the United States, it would stretch from the Atlantic Coast to the Pacific Coast. Valles Marineris is so huge that Earth's Grand Canyon could easily fit into one of its smaller side canyons.

▶ Where Did All the Water Go?

Geologic evidence in many parts of Mars indicates that liquid water may have once existed on the surface of the Red Planet. Indeed, many landforms suggest that Mars was once subjected to massive flooding. There are huge channels that cut deeply into volcanic

This view of Mars, made from images combined to present a global picture, features the huge canyon system known as the Valles Marineris, or Mariner Valley, at the center. It is the largest canyon system in the solar system.

plains. Some channels extend for thousands of miles. These channels are not the straight-line canali observed by Schiaparelli and Lowell, but resemble dried-up river channels. Some channels form valley networks in the highlands, similar to those created by streams on Earth. Teardrop-shaped landforms are probably the result of ancient flooding and erosion by huge volumes of water. So where did all the water go?

Because the air on Mars is so thin, the surface of the planet has no liquid water. (The thinner the air, the lower the boiling point of water.) On Mars, the boiling point of water is not much above the freezing point. So liquid water on the surface of Mars would quickly boil away. Any surface water that did not evaporate would freeze. Many scientists believe that there is water on Mars, but it is not in liquid form and therefore hard to find. They think that most of the water on Mars exists today as permafrost, ice frozen beneath the ground, in the lowlands of the northern hemisphere. They also believe that permafrost and groundwater may exist in the cratered highlands of the southern hemisphere. They do know that the northern polar cap contains water in the form of ice.

Liquid water is believed to be necessary for life. If liquid water did exist on the surface of Mars, as evidence seems to suggest, then the Red Planet must have been a warmer world at one time.

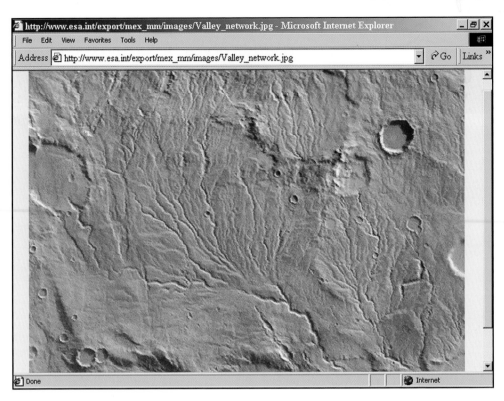

▲ *Networks of valleys on Mars suggest to scientists that rivers once existed on the planet.*

Conditions there may once have been suitable for life to emerge. If Mars was once warmer and wetter, why it became colder and drier remains a mystery. Scientists think they may have found conclusive geological evidence that Mars had liquid water as they continue to search for signs of life on the Red Planet.

Chapter 3 ▶

The Movements of Mars

The planet Mars orbits the Sun at an average distance of about 142 million miles (228 million kilometers). Because Mars is about one and a half times farther away from the Sun than Earth is, it takes much longer than Earth to complete one revolution around the Sun. While Earth travels around the Sun at a velocity of about 19 miles per second (31 kilometers per second), Mars moves at only 15 miles per second (24 kilometers per second). And Mars has a much longer journey. So it takes Mars 687 Earth days to orbit the Sun, while it takes Earth 365 days, or one year, to do that. The length of a year on Mars is almost twice as long as a year on Earth.

But a Martian day is almost the same length as a day on Earth because Mars rotates on its axis once in 24 hours 39 minutes. Mars's axis is tilted at about 24 degrees, almost the same as the 23.5-degree tilt of Earth's axis. So, like Earth, Mars has four seasons. But on Mars, each season lasts about twice as long as seasons on Earth do because Mars's orbital period is longer.

▶ From Perihelion to Aphelion

For thousands of years, the movements of Mars as it journeyed across the heavens puzzled those who carefully observed the planet. At times, it seemed to change speed and direction as it appeared to slow down, stop, and then reverse course. Perhaps that is why the ancient Egyptians called Mars "the backward traveler."

Two thousand years ago, Ptolemy came up with a complex and clever system to make Mars's strange movements fit into his Earth-centered view of the universe. He spoke of "epicycles" and "eccentrics" to explain how his system worked. According

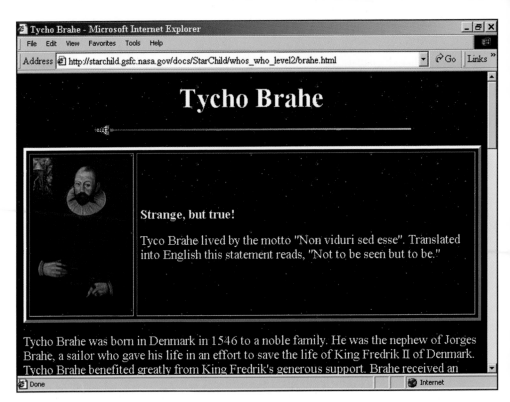

Tycho Brahe

Strange, but true!

Tyco Brahe lived by the motto "Non viduri sed esse". Translated into English this statement reads, "Not to be seen but to be."

Tycho Brahe was born in Denmark in 1546 to a noble family. He was the nephew of Jorges Brahe, a sailor who gave his life in an effort to save the life of King Fredrik II of Denmark. Tycho Brahe benefited greatly from King Fredrik's generous support. Brahe received an

🗐 Done   🌐 Internet

△ *The sixteenth-century Danish astronomer Tycho Brahe made detailed observations of Mars and the other planets without the benefit of a telescope. His data helped the German astronomer Johannes Kepler solve the mystery of Mars's elliptical orbit.*

to Ptolemy, as Mars was orbiting Earth in a circle, it also made mini-orbits around moving centers as it traveled around Earth. We now know that Ptolemy's ingenious ideas were totally wrong. Eventually, Copernicus' heliocentric model of the solar system replaced the geocentric model of Ptolemy. But Copernicus' system failed to explain the strange movements of Mars. When Earth, the faster of the two, approaches and then overtakes Mars as the two planets journey around the Sun, Mars seems to move backward for a time.

In 1609, the German astronomer Johannes Kepler solved the puzzle of Mars's motion. Kepler was a strong believer in

Copernicus' ideas. Using the naked-eye observations of Mars by Danish astronomer Tycho Brahe, Kepler recognized that Mars's backward motion was an illusion. Kepler realized that the apparent puzzling movements of Mars are caused by the differences in the orbital speeds of Earth and Mars. He determined that Mars follows an elliptical, or oval, path around the Sun rather than a circular one and moves in a predictable motion. Kepler then found that *all* the planets move around the Sun in elliptical orbits rather than in perfect circles. He also discovered that the planets move faster when they are closest to the Sun in their orbital journeys.

Mars provided the key to Kepler's discoveries, because its elliptical orbit is more eccentric or extreme than those of most of the other planets. The orbit of Venus, for example, is only slightly elliptical. And whereas the difference between Earth's least and greatest distances from the Sun is about 4 million miles (6 million kilometers), the figure for Mars is more than 25 million miles (40 million kilometers). At perihelion, its closest point to the Sun, Mars is 128 million miles (206 million kilometers) away. Mars is about 155 million miles (249 million kilometers) away from the Sun at aphelion, its farthest point from the Sun.[1]

Chapter 4 ▶

The Mysterious Moons of Mars

Unlike Earth and its one large Moon, Mars has two tiny moons. The Martian moons are so small and reflect so little light that they were not discovered until 1877 by the American astronomer Asaph Hall. He named them Phobos (Greek for "fear") and Deimos (Greek for "terror"), who were the two servants of Ares, the Greek god of war.

▷ Phobos and Deimos

Both Martian moons are irregularly shaped dark, lumpy rocks that orbit the Red Planet from west to east—the same direction that Mars rotates. Phobos is the larger of the two. But this tiny moon is only about 13 miles (21 kilometers) wide at its widest point. Phobos is covered with craters like those on Earth's Moon. The largest crater is 6 miles (10 kilometers) wide, about one third of the size of the satellite itself. The crater is named Stickney after Chloe Angeline Stickney Hall, Asaph Hall's wife, who had also been his mathematics professor in college. She encouraged her husband to continue searching for the moons of Mars when he was about to give up. There are grooves on the moon's surface that may have been caused by the object that blasted out the Stickney Crater.

Phobos is very close to the Martian surface, only 3,700 miles (5,953 kilometers) away. In the future it will be even closer to Mars. Scientists believe Phobos is slowly moving closer to Mars and that in about 50 million years, it will crash into the planet. If a person were standing on Phobos, Mars would fill nearly half the sky he or she saw. Phobos orbits Mars in about seven hours and thirty-nine minutes, always keeping the same face turned toward

This is one of the latest ▶
photographs of the tiny Martian
moon known as Phobos.

This is one of the latest ▶ photographs of the tiny Martian moon known as Phobos.

the planet. To someone standing on Mars, Phobos would appear to rise in the west two times a day.

Tiny Deimos is only 7 miles (11.3 kilometers) across. It is 12,500 miles (20,113 kilometers) from the surface of Mars. Deimos orbits Mars in about thirty hours and eighteen minutes. It appears to rise in the east and takes two and a half days to cross the sky before it sets. There are many craters on the surface of Deimos, but fewer than on Phobos.

▷ Jonathan Swift, Voltaire, and the Martian Moons

In Jonathan Swift's story "The Voyage to Laputa," published in 1727, the character Dr. Lemuel Gulliver visits Laputa, an island in the sky. There he learns that Laputan astronomers have "discovered two lesser stars, or satellites, which revolve about Mars, whereof the innermost is distant from the centre of the primary planet exactly three of its diameters, and the outermost five; the former revolves in the space of ten hours, and the latter in twenty-one and a half. . . ."[1] Phobos and Deimos had not been seen until Asaph Hall discovered them in 1877. So how did Swift know in 1727 that Mars has two moons? Was it just a good guess on his part or an amazing coincidence? Or something more mysterious?

In Voltaire's novel *Micromégas,* published in 1752, a being from the star Sirius visits the solar system. According to this being, "Our travellers crossed a space of about a hundred million leagues and reached the planet Mars. They saw two moons which wait on this planet, and which have escaped the gaze of astronomers. . . . How difficult it would be for Mars, which is so far from the sun, to get on with less than two moons!"[2] Now, how could Voltaire have known about the two moons of Mars? Had he simply read Swift's story?

The answer is that most likely Swift, and probably Voltaire and many others, had some knowledge of the ideas of Johannes Kepler. And Kepler, as early as 1610, had predicted that Mars must have two satellites. Kepler was a firm believer in mathematical laws governing the heavenly bodies and their orbits. As far as he knew, Mercury and Venus, the first and second planets from the Sun, had no moons. Earth, the third planet, had one Moon. Kepler learned that Galileo had observed four moons revolving around Jupiter, the fifth planet. So Kepler reasoned that Mars, the fourth planet from the Sun, must have two moons. Today the two most prominent craters on the Martian moon Deimos are named Swift and Voltaire.

▷ Mars's Two Satellites—Natural or Artificial?

Where did Mars's two moons come from? Many scientists believe that Phobos and Deimos were asteroids that wandered too close to Mars and were captured by the planet's gravitational field. Other scientists theorize that the two moons may actually have formed from a buildup of material left over after the formation of Mars. The trouble with this theory is that the two satellites are very different in color and density than Mars.

One scientist had a totally different theory. In 1960, after studying all that was known about the motion of Phobos, a respected Soviet astrophysicist named Iosif S. Shklovskii came to the conclusion that the satellite must be extremely light. Shklovskii went on to wonder how a natural rocky satellite could possibly be so light. He speculated that perhaps it was actually hollow—and no satellite of that size could be hollow and natural.

Deimos, the other moon of Mars, ▷
features a heavily cratered surface.

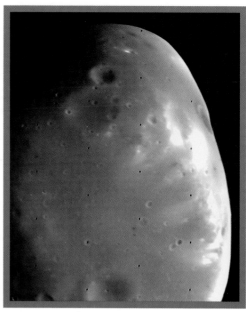

Therefore, it would have to be an artificial satellite, the product of a Martian civilization far more advanced than our own. In *Intelligent Life in the Universe,* which he cowrote with Carl Sagan, Shklovskii talks about this theory that Mars's moons might actually be space stations:

> Since Mars does not have a large natural satellite such as our moon, the construction of large, artificial satellites would be of relatively greater importance to an advanced Martian civilization in its expansion into space. . . . Perhaps Phobos was launched into orbit in the heyday of a technical civilization on Mars, some hundreds of millions of years ago.[3]

He concluded that the other Martian moon, Deimos, was probably also an artificial satellite.

In August 1969, close-up photos of Phobos and Deimos sent back to Earth by the *Mariner 7* space probe put an end to Shklovskii's interesting theory. They showed that the moons of Mars were not spherical or cylindrical, nor did they have a shiny metallic appearance. In no way could they be mistaken for space stations. Phobos and Deimos were just dark, lumpy pieces of rock with highly irregular shapes, and Phobos was described by some scientists as looking like "a diseased potato."[4]

Chapter 5

Exploring Mars

Spurred on by the Soviet Union's successful launch of *Sputnik 1,* an unmanned satellite that orbited Earth in 1957, the United States entered a space race with its superpower rival. During the course of the competition, both sides claimed major breakthroughs. In 1961, the Soviets were the first to send a human being into space, although in 1969, the United States became the first to land astronauts on the Moon.

While most of the world's attention was focused on the amazing exploits of brave astronauts and cosmonauts, impressive progress was also occurring in American and Soviet unmanned space programs. Both countries launched unmanned space probes to Venus, Mars, and more distant planets throughout the 1960s and the decades that followed.

▶ Unmanned Space Missions to Mars: Mariner and Viking

Although the Soviets were the first to launch a spacecraft to Mars, the mission was not very successful. In November 1962, the Soviet *Mars 1* space probe flew by the Red Planet but failed to send back any useful data. The United States went on to have more success on Mars than the Soviet Union. The National Aeronautics and Space Administration (NASA) began a long series of space missions to Mars, which provided a wealth of new information about the Red Planet.

In July 1965, *Mariner 4,* the first successful American mission to Mars, flew within 6,118 miles (9,846 kilometers) of the Red Planet. It sent back twenty-two black-and-white images of a heavily cratered portion of the Martian surface that resembled

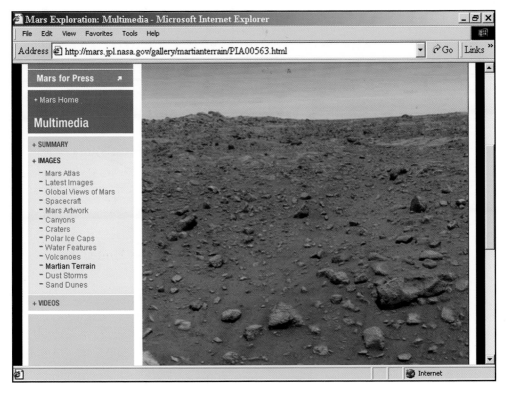

Mars Exploration: Multimedia - Microsoft Internet Explorer	_ 🗗 ✕

File   Edit   View   Favorites   Tools   Help

Address 🔲 http://mars.jpl.nasa.gov/gallery/martianterrain/PIA00563.html   ▾   𝒫 Go   Links »

Mars for Press ↗

+ Mars Home

Multimedia

+ SUMMARY

+ IMAGES
- Mars Atlas
- Latest Images
- Global Views of Mars
- Spacecraft
- Mars Artwork
- Canyons
- Craters
- Polar Ice Caps
- Water Features
- Volcanoes
- **Martian Terrain**
- Dust Storms
- Sand Dunes

+ VIDEOS

🔲 Internet

▲ *On July 21, 1976, the day after* Viking 1 *successfully landed on Mars, this first color photograph of the Martian surface revealed a reddish-orange material covering most of the land.*

the surface of our own Moon. *Mariner 6* flew within 2,130 miles (3,430 kilometers) of Mars in July 1969. One month later, *Mariner 7* reached Mars. The two probes sent back nearly two hundred images.

In November 1971, *Mariner 9* became the first space probe to orbit another planet when it reached Mars. A planet-wide dust storm cleared after a few weeks, and *Mariner 9* sent back 7,329 images of the surface of Mars. Among them were images of Mars's gigantic volcanoes. There were also images of what appeared to be ancient riverbeds. *Mariner 9* confirmed that there was no liquid water on the surface of Mars. Scientists studying the photos also solved the mystery of the dark areas on the planet's surface that

▲ On July 20, 1976, the Viking 1 spacecraft, whose lander is pictured, was the first to successfully touch down on the surface of Mars. The Viking 2 lander followed on September 3 of that year. The two landers transmitted images of the Martian surface and analyzed samples of its soil.

seemed to change color with the seasons. Earlier astronomers had first believed these areas to be seas. Later, some astronomers believed the areas to consist of vegetation. But scientists could see that they were actually areas of windblown dust rearranged by seasonal winds.

The next goal in the exploration of Mars was to land a spacecraft on the planet's surface. The best chance for success would be to send an orbiter that carried a lander. The orbiter could identify suitable landing sites and then release the lander for its trip to the surface. In June 1976, *Viking 1* went into orbit around Mars. It sent images of possible landing sites to mission controllers on Earth. Then on July 20, it became the first lander to successfully land on Mars when it touched down on the planet's surface in an area called Chryse Planitia. Almost immediately, *Viking 1* began sending back the first images from the surface of Mars. Excited scientists back on Earth marveled at Martian rocks and boulders strewn across a desolate red desert beneath a pink sky. Images of the Martian landscape kept coming.

Meanwhile, *Viking 2* went into orbit around Mars in August 1976, and its lander touched down on Mars on September 3 in an area called Utopia Planitia. The *Viking 1* orbiter continued operating until 1980, and the *Viking 2* orbiter ceased operating in 1978. Both produced detailed maps of most of Mars's surface. The Viking landers gathered data about the weather. Chemical analyses of soil samples near the landing sites revealed no evidence of life. The *Viking 1* lander sent its last transmission in 1982, and the *Viking 2* lander was turned off in 1980.

Pathfinder, Global Surveyor, and Odyssey

On July 4, 1997, the Mars *Pathfinder* space probe landed on the Red Planet in an area called Ares Vallis. *Pathfinder* sent back color photos and information about wind speed, temperature, and air pressure on Mars. The erosion of rocks in the area suggested that the dusty Ares Vallis had once been a vast flood plain with floodwaters flowing over it. *Pathfinder* came equipped with a robotic rover called *Sojourner*, a 23-pound, 6-wheeled robot that looked like a toy car. *Sojourner* explored the Martian surface within 30 feet (9 meters) of the lander for thirty Martian days. The rover was controlled by a scientist at NASA's Mission Control Center in Houston, Texas. *Sojourner* explored two hills, named "Twin Peaks" by the scientists, who believed they were shaped by flowing water.

Part of the Mars Pathfinder lander and a deflated air bag form the bottom of this panoramic image of the Martian hills dubbed "Twin Peaks" by scientists.

In September 1997, the Mars *Global Surveyor* went into orbit around Mars. In 1998, scientists used the Mars Orbiter Laser Altimeter (MOLA) aboard the *Global Surveyor* to make three-dimensional photographs and a map of Mars's north pole. By 2002, the *Global Surveyor* had sent 100,000 photos back to Earth. It is still orbiting the planet. In April 2001, the Mars *Odyssey* was launched and arrived in orbit around Mars in 2002. It began photomapping the planet and identifying minerals and chemical elements on the surface. The *Odyssey* also identified where water ice lies buried beneath the surface of Mars. The orbiters continue to serve the important function of relaying messages sent from landers on Mars's surface to scientists back on Earth.

Mars Exploration Rover . . . and Beyond

In January 2004, NASA's Mars Exploration Rover (MER) mission, with its twin vehicles *Spirit* and *Opportunity,* arrived on Mars. On January 3, *Spirit* landed in the Gusev Crater just north of the Martian equator and beamed back spectacular three-dimensional images of the surrounding landscape. The six-wheeled *Spirit* rover began navigating the crater in search of evidence that water once flowed there. On January 24, *Opportunity* landed at Meridiani Planum, a flat plain just south of the Martian equator, almost exactly on the other side of the planet.

The Mars Exploration Rovers have carried out analyses of rock and soil samples. *Spirit* dug a small trench in the Martian soil and detected the presence of magnesium-sulfate salts. Scientists believe it is possible that water percolated from underground, dissolving out minerals. As the water evaporated near the surface, it left the concentrated salts behind. The rover *Opportunity* discovered the presence of sulfates in rocks, helping make the case for a watery history. The rovers also discovered hematite, chlorine, and bromine in rocks. These minerals probably indicate the presence of liquid water.

NASA's scientists will continue their search for evidence of life on Mars with missions planned through 2015. In August 2005, NASA plans to launch the Mars *Reconnaissance Orbiter.* It will be equipped with the most powerful camera ever flown to another planet. The camera, capable of sending back clear images of objects as small as a dinner plate, will enable scientists to study the surface of Mars in amazing detail. Then in August 2007, NASA will launch the *Phoenix* mission to the northern polar region of Mars. Its sophisticated instruments will dig down through the layers of water ice. Scientists believe it is possible that these layers could contain organic compounds that are necessary for life.

Future unmanned missions to Mars will collect rock and soil samples and return them to Earth for study by humans rather than by robots. Scientists who analyze these samples will be eagerly looking for fossil microbes. By 2009, NASA hopes to launch the Mars *Science Laboratory* and the Mars *Telecommunications Orbiter* to pave the way for a sample return mission. The first sample return mission will be launched between 2011 and 2016.

Is There Life on Mars?

While scientists have not yet found any evidence of life on the Red Planet, they also have not given up hope that some form of life existed—or may even still exist—there. During the summer

▲ *The future of Martian exploration includes a proposed NASA mission known as the Mars Science Laboratory, slated for a 2009 launch. This rover will be designed to investigate a greater range of Martian soil and rocks than any previous Mars rover.*

of 1976, early in the Viking missions, there was a great deal of excitement when scientists received "false-positive" readings from Mars that seemed to point to the existence of active life on the Red Planet. Later, however, scientists realized these readings were not accurate after they had found out more about the surface chemistry of Mars.

Scientists have since changed their thinking about life on Mars partly because they have found life on Earth in places where they did not think it could exist. In 2000, scientists reported evidence of bacteria in 250-million-year-old terrestrial salt crystals.[1] Other scientists discovered living bacteria in ice deep below the

Antarctic ice cap. The soil on Mars is believed to be sterile because the surface of the planet is sterilized by solar ultraviolet radiation. But could microbes exist on Mars underground or inside of rocks?

In 1984, scientists found a 4-pound (2-kilogram) meteorite in Antarctica. They determined that the meteorite, which they named ALH 84001, had originated on Mars. They believe that about 3.6 billion years ago, a large asteroid slammed into Mars with enough force to blast chunks of Martian rock into space. The rocks went into orbit around the Sun, and at times, some rocks became dislodged from their orbits. This particular rock reached Earth and fell on Antarctica as a meteorite. Scientists were amazed when they discovered tiny worm-shaped structures inside cracks in the meteorite. Some scientists believe the structures are fossils of primitive microbes, although other scientists doubt that theory.

A "Face" on Mars

Imagine the excitement that any evidence of intelligent life on Mars would create. On July 25, 1976, the *Viking 1* orbiter, while searching for a landing site for *Viking 2,* photographed what appeared to be a mile-wide sculpture of a human face on the surface of Mars. If this were truly a human face, it would be the most astounding discovery in human history. The "face" is in the Cydonia region of Mars. UFO watchers and many others were convinced that the face on Mars was an artificial construction. When NASA scientists said the face was just a chance arrangement of hills and rocks, believers in the face accused NASA of a cover-up.

For more than twenty years, some people wondered who had created the square-jawed, tight-lipped face. Then on April 5, 1998, the Mars *Global Surveyor* sent back a new image of the face. This time the light was coming from a different direction and showed that the face was just an eroded mesa, a mostly flat-topped elevated natural surface. The facelike pattern had been

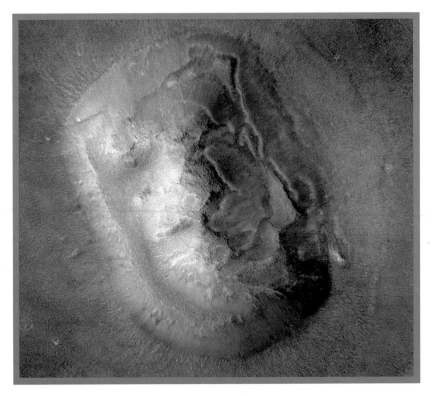

In 2001, a camera on the Mars Global Surveyor captured this image of the "face" on Mars in the planet's Cydonia region. According to NASA scientists, this mesa's shadows are what create the resemblance to a human face. There are still those who believe that this is an actual creation of intelligent beings.

produced by shadows. Some true believers rejected the new image as just one more attempt at a cover-up by NASA.

In the years to come, there will indeed be faces on Mars if NASA succeeds in its plans to send a manned expedition to Mars. Only, those faces will be the faces of humans who have finally been able to journey to the Red Planet.

aphelion—The point in a planet's or other celestial body's path when it is farthest from the Sun.

asteroid—A rocky body in space that orbits the Sun.

geocentric model—A model of the solar system that has Earth at its center.

heliocentric model—A model of the solar system that has the Sun at its center.

ice cap—A large and thick mass of ice and snow that permanently covers land.

impact crater—A circular depression made in the surface of a planet or moon when a meteorite crashes into it.

meteor—An object made of rock or ice that travels through space and enters Earth's atmosphere.

meteorite—A rock from space that has traveled through Earth's atmosphere and fallen to the ground.

microbes—Microorganisms, or organisms so small that they can only be seen through a microscope.

perihelion—The point in a planet's or other celestial body's path when it is closest to the Sun.

photomapping—The process of taking photographs of an area from above and applying a grid and other data to the photographs to produce a map.

terrestrial—Of Earth or like Earth; Mars, Venus, Mercury, and Earth are classified as terrestrial planets because they have similar densities and compositions.

Chapter 1. The Red Planet

1. John Noble Wilford, *Mars Beckons: The Mysteries, the Challenges, the Expectations of Our Next Great Adventure in Space* (New York: Alfred A. Knopf, 1990), p. 8.

2. Jeff Rovin, *Mars!* (Los Angeles: Corwin Books, 1978), p. 38.

3. Wilford, p. 9.

4. Paul Raeburn, *Uncovering the Secrets of the Red Planet: Mars* (Washington, D.C.: The National Geographic Society, 1998), p. 34.

5. Patrick Moore, *On Mars* (London: Cassell, 1998), p. 35.

6. Wilford, p. 15.

7. Ibid., p. 23.

8. Ibid., p. 31.

9. Ibid., p. 32.

10. Ibid., p. 30.

Chapter 2. Our Cold, Dry Neighbor

1. Thomas R. Watters, *Planets: A Smithsonian Guide* (New York: Macmillan, 1995), p. 60.

2. Ibid., p. 121.

Chapter 3. The Movements of Mars

1. Patrick Moore, *On Mars* (London: Cassell, 1998), p. 19.

Chapter 4. The Mysterious Moons of Mars

1. Jeff Rovin, *Mars!* (Los Angeles: Corwin Books, 1978), p. 40.

2. John Noble Wilford, *Mars Beckons: The Mysteries, the Challenges, the Expectations of Our Next Great Adventure in Space* (New York: Alfred A. Knopf, 1990), p. 72.

3. I.S. Shklovskii and Carl Sagan, *Intelligent Life in the Universe* (New York: Dell Publishing Company, 1966), pp. 376–377.

4. Paul Raeburn, *Uncovering the Secrets of the Red Planet: Mars* (Washington, D.C.: The National Geographic Society, 1998), p. 103.

Chapter 5. Exploring Mars

1. William K. Hartmann, *A Traveler's Guide to Mars: The Mysterious Landscapes of the Red Planet* (New York: Workman Publishing, 2003), p. 424.

Asimov, Isaac, with revisions and updating by Richard Hantula. *Mars*. Milwaukee: Gareth Stevens, 2002.

Cole, Michael D. *Mars—The Fourth Planet*. Berkeley Heights, N.J.: Enslow Publishers, Inc., 2002.

Davis, Lucile. *The Mars Rovers*. San Diego: Kidhaven Press, 2004.

Getz, David. *Life on Mars*. New York: Henry Holt & Co., 2004.

Gifford, Clive. *How to Live on Mars*. New York: Franklin Watts, 2001.

Krull, Kathleen. *The Night the Martians Landed: Just the Facts (Plus the Rumors) About Invaders From Mars*. New York: HarperCollins, 2003.

Miller, Ron. *Mars*. Brookfield, Conn.: Twenty-First Century Books, 2004.

Ride, Sally, and Tam O'Shaughnessy. *Exploring Our Solar System*. New York: Crown Publishers, Inc., 2003.

Simon, Seymour. *Destination: Mars*. New York: HarperCollins, 2000.

Vogt, Gregory. *Mars*. Austin, Tex.: Steadwell Books, 2001.